Overcoming The Bruise within

(Turning Trauma Into Triumph)

Kevin Graham

Copyright © 2023 Kevin Graham
All rights reserved.
ISBN: 9798864327708

DEDICATION

To all those silently suffering,

This dedication is for you, the brave souls who have carried the weight of unhealed and unhealthy emotions in the depths of your being. It is a recognition of the battles fought within, hidden from the world, as you navigate the complexities of life under the shadow of pain.

This book is a beacon of hope, a guiding light on your path towards healing, recovery, and transformation. It is a testament to your resilience, for despite the invisible struggles you face, you have persevered. You have shown incredible strength, even when it felt like the weight of the world was too much to bear.

Within these pages, you will find solace, understanding, and the tools to embark on a journey of self-discovery. It is a testament to the power of vulnerability, as you confront the darkest corners of your soul, acknowledge the wounds that have shaped you, and begin the process of healing.

May this book serve as a companion, offering insights and wisdom that resonate with your unique experiences. May it provide a safe space for you to explore your emotions, confront your fears, and find the strength to move forward.

Remember, you are not alone. Countless others have walked similar paths, and their stories of triumph over adversity are woven into the fabric of these pages. Let their experiences inspire you, and let their victories remind you that healing is possible.

Embrace this opportunity to reclaim your life, to shed the burdens that have held you back, and to step into a future filled with hope and happiness. You deserve every ounce of joy that life has to offer, and this book is a testament to that truth.

With unwavering support, compassion, and empathy, this book is dedicated to you, the courageous souls who have endured in silence. May it be a catalyst for your transformation, a roadmap to healing, and a reminder that you are worthy of love, happiness, and a life free from the shackles of unprocessed emotions.

You are seen, you are heard, and you are not alone. With love and warmth,

Kevin Graham

Table of Contents

ACKNOWLEDGMENTS 1

CHAPTER 1: Understanding Emotional Bruises: The Power of Inner Wounds 4

    Section 1: Defining Emotional Bruises 4

    1.1 The Correlation with Physical Bruises 4

    1.2 Emotions as Bruises 5

    Section 2: Signs and Symptoms of Emotional Bruises 5

    2.1 Mind Bruises 5

    Section 2: Signs and Symptoms of Emotional Bruises 5

    2.1 Mind Bruises 5

    2.2 Heart Bruises 7

    Section 3: The Power of Inner Wounds 10

    3.1 Impact on Daily Life 10

    Section 4: Journal Reflection 12

    2 Trauma 14

    Worksheet: Manifestation of Broken Heart in Relationship with God 16

    3 HIDDEN IN PLAIN SIGHT 22

    4 EMOTIONAL IRRIGATION 32

    (WOUND CLEANSING) 32

    5 THE ANATOMY OF AN OVERCOME 39

    6 USING THE F WORD 46

    Prayer of Release 53

    Heavenly Father, ... 53

ABOUT THE AUTHOR 54

ACKNOWLEDGMENTS

I would like to express my deepest gratitude to my mother, Louia Graham. Your unwavering resilience in the face of life's adversities has been an endless source of inspiration for me. Your strength has given me the courage to endure even the most challenging times. I am forever grateful for your love, support, and the invaluable life lessons you have taught me.

I would also like to extend my heartfelt appreciation to my brother, Keith Graham. Your unwavering belief in my abilities has been a constant source of encouragement. Your unwavering faith in me has given me the confidence to face my fears and overcome obstacles. Thank you for always being there for me and for teaching me the importance of self-belief.

To my beloved wife, Monica Graham, and our precious children, I cannot find the words to express how profoundly grateful I am to have you in my life. Your love, companionship, and unwavering support have made every moment of my existence meaningful and worthwhile. You have been my rock, my source of joy, and my reason to strive for greatness. Life has been truly extraordinary with you by my side, and I cherish every precious memory we have created together.

To all the incredible individuals who have touched my life and contributed to my journey, your presence and influence have shaped me into who I am today. Thank you for your love, guidance, and unwavering support.

1. emotional bruises

Once upon a time, in a small town tucked away in the countryside, there lived a young girl named Emily. She grew up in a household filled with emotionally unavailable adults, where love and affection seemed like distant concepts. The adults in her life carried their own burdens and traumas, leaving little room for them to tend to the emotional needs of a young child.

As Emily navigated her way through childhood, she couldn't help but internalize the belief that she was the cause of the various dysfunctions within her family. Her young mind struggled to understand why she couldn't elicit the love and attention she so desperately craved. The weight of her perceived inadequacy, coupled with the absence of emotional support, began to take its toll.

Trauma, like an invisible force, weaved its way into Emily's life, creating a false narrative within her mind. Unable to process the psychological and emotional wounds derived from feelings of abandonment, isolation, and shame, she carried these burdens deep within her. The bruises of her experiences were hidden beneath a carefully constructed facade, unseen by the outside world.

In a society that often focuses on the external, it is easy to overlook the internal battles that many face. Just as bruises are only seen on the surface, the invisible wounds of emotional turmoil often go undetected until they manifest in outward ways. Emily's brokenness remained hidden, tucked away beneath a smile that masked her pain.

But as life unfolded, Emily's internal bleeding could no longer be ignored. It began to seep through the cracks, staining her interactions and relationships. She found herself struggling to form deep connections with others, guarded by the fear of rejection and abandonment that had become so ingrained within her.

Recognizing the need to heal, Emily embarked on a journey of self-discovery and growth. She sought out therapy, where she learned to unravel the tangled web of emotions that had plagued her for so long. Through introspection and guidance, Emily began to understand that she was not the cause of her family's dysfunction. She learned to separate her own self-worth from the actions and limitations of others.

Beneath the surface, Emily discovered the power to confront her past and rewrite her narrative. She allowed herself to feel the pain, to mourn the loss of the nurturing she had longed for, and to release the shame that was never hers to carry. With every step forward, she washed away the root causes of her internal bleeding, finding solace in the knowledge that healing was possible.

Emily's journey was not without its challenges, but with time, patience, and self-compassion, her emotional bruises began to fade. The brokenness that once defined her existence transformed into resilience and strength. And as she continued to heal, she made a vow to herself – a vow to break the cycle and create a nurturing environment for those who would come after her.

In the end, Emily's story served as a reminder that the bruises we carry within are just as real as those we can see with our eyes. They deserve attention, care, and understanding. And with the willingness to confront our inner battles, we can wash away the root causes of our pain and find the healing and freedom we deserve.

CHAPTER 1

Understanding Emotional Bruises: The Power of Inner Wounds

Introduction:

Emotions are an integral part of our human experience. They shape our perceptions, influence our behavior, and provide us with valuable insights into our inner world. Just as physical bruises indicate injuries to our body, emotional bruises signify wounds within our mind and heart. In this chapter, we will delve into the concept of emotional bruises, exploring their correlation with physical bruises, discussing signs and symptoms, and reflecting on the impact they have on our lives.

Section 1: Defining Emotional Bruises

1.1 The Correlation with Physical Bruises

- Just as physical bruises result from external forces impacting our body, emotional bruises are the result of internal or external factors affecting our mind and heart.
- While physical bruises are visible on the surface, emotional bruises are often hidden and can be challenging to identify or acknowledge.

1.2 Emotions as Bruises

- Emotions serve as indicators of our psychological well-being, much like bruises signal physical injury.
- Emotional bruises can be caused by various factors such as traumatic experiences, unresolved conflicts, unmet needs, or prolonged stress.

Section 2: Signs and Symptoms of Emotional Bruises

2.1 Mind Bruises

- Persistent negative thoughts and self-criticism.
- Difficulty concentrating or making decisions.
- Heightened anxiety or fear.
- Decreased self-esteem and feelings of worthlessness.

Sure! Here's an interactive worksheet for Section 2: Signs and Symptoms of Emotional Bruises.

Section 2: Signs and Symptoms of Emotional Bruises

2.1 Mind Bruises

Please rate the following statements based on how often you experience them, using the scale:

0 - Never
1 - Rarely
2 - Sometimes
3 - Often
4 - Very often

1. Persistent negative thoughts and self-criticism.

    - How often do you experience persistent negative thoughts and self-criticism?
    - Rating: _____

2. Difficulty concentrating or making decisions.

    - How often do you experience difficulty concentrating or making decisions?
    - Rating: _____

3. Heightened anxiety or fear.

    - How often do you experience heightened anxiety or fear?
    - Rating: _____

4. Decreased self-esteem and feelings of worthlessness.

    - How often do you experience decreased self-esteem and feelings of worthlessness?
    - Rating: _____

Please take a moment to reflect on your ratings and consider the impact these signs and symptoms may have on your emotional well-being.

Remember, this worksheet is intended to help you become more aware of your emotions and identify potential areas for growth and healing. If you're experiencing significant distress or need professional assistance, please reach out to a mental health professional.

Feel free to continue to the next section or explore further signs and symptoms of emotional bruises.

2.2 Heart Bruises

- Intense sadness, grief, or hopelessness.
- Emotional numbness or detachment.
- Difficulty forming or maintaining intimate relationships.
- Trust issues and fear of vulnerability.

Heart Bruises Interactive Worksheet

Instructions:

Take a few moments to reflect on the following statements and consider how they relate to your own experiences. Rate each statement on a scale of 1 to 5, with 1 indicating "Not at all true for me" and 5 indicating "Very true for me." Be honest and authentic in your responses. Once you have rated each statement, we will discuss your results and explore ways to heal and nurture your heart.

Statement 1: Intense sadness, grief, or hopelessness.
Rate: 1 2 3 4 5

Statement 2: Emotional numbness or detachment.
Rate: 1 2 3 4 5

Statement 3: Difficulty forming or maintaining intimate relationships.
Rate: 1 2 3 4 5

Statement 4: Trust issues and fear of vulnerability.
Rate: 1 2 3 4 5

Discussion:

Now that you have rated each statement, let's explore your responses and discuss the impact of heart bruises on your emotional well-being.

1. Intense sadness, grief, or hopelessness:
    - How frequently do you experience intense sadness, grief, or hopelessness?
    - What are some situations or triggers that intensify these emotions for you?
    - How do these emotions affect your daily life and overall happiness?

2. Emotional numbness or detachment:
    - To what extent do you feel emotionally numb or detached?
    - Are there specific circumstances or events that contribute to this feeling?
    - How does emotional numbness or detachment impact your ability to connect with others and experience joy?

3. Difficulty forming or maintaining intimate relationships:
    - Have you noticed challenges in forming or maintaining intimate relationships?
    - What are some common difficulties you encounter in these relationships?
    - How do these challenges affect your sense of fulfillment and connection with others?

4. Trust issues and fear of vulnerability:
    - Do you struggle with trust issues or fear of vulnerability?
    - Are there past experiences that have contributed to these feelings?
    - How do trust issues and fear of vulnerability hinder your ability to develop deep and meaningful connections?

Healing and Nurturing:

Now that we have explored your responses, let's discuss strategies to heal and nurture your heart:

1. Seek support: Consider reaching out to a trusted friend, family member, or therapist who can provide a safe space for you to share your feelings and experiences.
2. Self-reflection: Take time to reflect on past experiences and identify any patterns or underlying causes for your heart bruises. This self-awareness can help you understand and address your emotional wounds.
3. Practice self-care: Engage in activities that bring you joy and help you relax. This may include exercise, hobbies, meditation, or spending time in nature.
4. Cultivate self-compassion: Be kind and gentle with yourself as you navigate the healing process. Treat yourself with the same understanding and compassion that you would offer to a close friend.
5. Professional help: If your heart bruises significantly impact your daily life or if you're struggling to cope, consider seeking professional help from a therapist or counselor who specializes in emotional healing and relationship issues.

Remember, healing takes time, and everyone's journey is unique. Be patient with yourself and allow yourself to heal at your own pace.

If you need further assistance or guidance, please don't hesitate to seek support from professionals or loved ones.

Section 3: The Power of Inner Wounds

3.1 Impact on Daily Life

- Emotional bruises can significantly impact our overall well-being and quality of life.
- They may manifest as behavioral patterns, such as avoidance, withdrawal, or self-sabotage.
- Emotional bruises can hinder personal growth, limit our potential, and create barriers to happiness and fulfillment.

Trauma can indeed manifest in multiple ways and have a significant impact on various aspects of a person's life, including their relationships. Two common manifestations of trauma that you mentioned are codependency and the lingering effects of childhood wounds. Let's explore each of these manifestations in more detail:

1. Codependency: Codependency refers to a dysfunctional relationship pattern where an individual excessively relies on another person for their sense of self-worth, identity, and emotional well-being. Codependency often emerges as a coping mechanism in response to trauma or an upbringing characterized by neglect, abuse, or inconsistent care. It can be seen as an attempt to regain control, security, and validation in relationships.

Codependent individuals may exhibit the following behaviors:

- Excessive caretaking: They may prioritize the needs of others while neglecting their own.
- Lack of boundaries: They have difficulty setting and enforcing personal boundaries, often merging their own identity with others.
- Low self-esteem: They may have a diminished sense of self-worth and rely on external validation for self-esteem.

- Fear of abandonment: They may have an intense fear of rejection or abandonment, leading to efforts to please others at all costs.
- Difficulty expressing emotions: They may struggle to identify and communicate their own emotions and needs.

2. Lingering effects of childhood wounds: Childhood experiences, particularly traumatic ones, can profoundly impact an individual's emotional and psychological development. Unresolved childhood wounds can affect relationships throughout a person's life, as they may struggle with trust, intimacy, and emotional regulation. Some common manifestations of childhood wounds include:

   - Trust issues: Individuals who have experienced trauma in childhood may find it challenging to trust others, leading to difficulties in forming and maintaining healthy relationships.
   - Fear of vulnerability: Childhood trauma can make it difficult for individuals to be emotionally vulnerable, as it may feel unsafe or threatening.
   - Emotional regulation difficulties: Traumatic experiences can disrupt the development of healthy coping mechanisms, leading to difficulties in managing and expressing emotions appropriately.
   - Patterns of reenactment: Unresolved childhood wounds can lead individuals to unconsciously seek out relationships that replicate familiar dynamics from their past, often perpetuating patterns of abuse, neglect, or dysfunction.
   - Attachment issues: Trauma can disrupt the formation of secure attachment styles, resulting in either an anxious-preoccupied attachment style (excessive need for validation and fear of abandonment) or an avoidant-dismissive attachment style (emotional distance and avoidance of intimacy).

It's important to note that while trauma can have a lasting impact on relationships, it is not a predetermined outcome. With awareness, support, and therapeutic interventions, individuals can heal from trauma, develop healthier relationship patterns, and cultivate more fulfilling connections with others.

3.2 Healing and Resilience

- Recognizing and acknowledging emotional bruises is an essential step towards healing.
- Developing resilience involves nurturing self-compassion, seeking support from loved ones or professionals, and engaging in therapeutic practices.
- Healing emotional bruises requires time, patience, and a commitment to self-care and self-reflection.

Section 4: Journal Reflection

Take a moment to reflect on the subject matter discussed in this chapter. Consider the following questions:

- Have you ever experienced emotional bruises in your life? If so, what were the circumstances surrounding them?
- How have emotional bruises impacted your thoughts, emotions, and behaviors?
- Are there any specific signs or symptoms you have noticed within yourself that may indicate the presence of emotional bruises?
- What steps can you take to begin the healing process and nurture resilience in the face of emotional bruises?

Use this journal reflection as an opportunity to delve deeper into your understanding of emotional bruises and to set intentions for your personal growth and healing journey.

Conclusion:

In this chapter, we have explored the concept of emotional bruises, drawing parallels with physical bruises, discussing signs and symptoms, and reflecting on the impact they have on our lives. Emotional bruises can be powerful teachers, urging us to pay attention to our inner wounds and take proactive steps towards healing and growth. By cultivating self-awareness and practicing self-care, we can embark on a transformative journey towards

2 Trauma

Introduction:

Trauma is a powerful force that permeates human existence, leaving profound impacts on individuals and societies alike. Within theological discourse, trauma can be interpreted as a rupture in the human experience brought about by the brokenness of the world. This chapter delves into the theological understanding of trauma, its disruptive effects on the fundamental aspects of human existence, and the profound emotional wounds it leaves behind.

Theological Interpretation of Trauma:

Within theological frameworks, trauma can be seen as a consequence of the fallen nature of the world, a result of the brokenness and sin that permeates human existence. Theological perspectives often acknowledge that God's original design for creation was one of harmony, where humanity lived in perfect communion with God, self, others, and the natural world. However, trauma disrupts this harmony, causing a rupture in the interconnectedness between these fundamental aspects.

Disruption of Safety, Trust, and Meaning:

Traumatic events shatter an individual's sense of safety, trust, and meaning. In moments of trauma, the world suddenly becomes a hostile and unpredictable place. The sense of security one once had is shattered, leading to a profound loss of trust in oneself, others, and even in the divine. Trauma strips away the meaning and coherence that individuals find in their lives, leaving them grappling with profound existential questions.

Disruption of Safety, Trust, and Meaning

Instructions: Answer the following questions based on your understanding of the disruption of safety, trust, and meaning caused by traumatic events.

1. Define the concept of safety in the context of traumatic events.
2. How does a traumatic event affect an individual's sense of safety?
3. Explain the role of trust in an individual's life and relationships.
4. In what ways can a traumatic event disrupt an individual's trust in oneself?
5. How does a traumatic event impact an individual's trust in others?
6. Discuss the potential effects of trauma on an individual's trust in the divine or higher power.
7. What is the significance of meaning in an individual's life?
8. How does a traumatic event challenge or disrupt an individual's sense of meaning?
9. Describe the existential questions that individuals may grapple with following a traumatic event.
10. Provide examples or scenarios to illustrate the disruption of safety, trust, and meaning caused by traumatic events.
11. Reflect on your own experiences or observations of how traumatic events can shatter safety, trust, and meaning in individuals' lives.
12. Suggest strategies or approaches that can help individuals rebuild safety, trust, and meaning after experiencing trauma.

Note: This worksheet is designed to facilitate reflection and understanding of the impact of traumatic events on safety, trust, and meaning. Take your time to answer each question thoughtfully and consider seeking professional support if you or someone you know has experienced trauma and requires assistance.

Impact on Relationship with God:

Trauma can significantly impact an individual's relationship with God. In moments of suffering and trauma, individuals may question the goodness, justice, or even the existence of God. The rupture caused by trauma can lead to feelings of abandonment, anger, and spiritual desolation. Individuals may struggle to reconcile their pain with their understanding of a loving and compassionate deity, thus further intensifying their emotional wounds.

Worksheet: Manifestation of Broken Heart in Relationship with God

Instructions:

Take some time to reflect on your own experiences and feelings regarding your relationship with God in the context of trauma or suffering. Use the following prompts to guide your reflection. Write down your responses in the spaces provided. Be honest and open with yourself as you explore your emotions and thoughts. Remember that this is a personal exercise, and there are no right or wrong answers.

1. Describe a specific traumatic experience or period of suffering that has had a significant impact on your relationship with God.

Traumatic experience or period of suffering: _____

2. How did this experience make you feel about God? (Check all that apply)

   - Abandoned
   - Angry
   - Confused
   - Betrayed
   - Doubtful of God's existence
   - Questioning God's goodness or justice

- Spiritually desolate
- Other: _____

3. In what ways has this trauma affected your ability to trust God or believe in His love and compassion? Explain.

_____
_____
_____

4. Have you sought answers or guidance from religious or spiritual sources to help you understand or cope with your trauma? If yes, describe your experience. If no, explain why.

_____
_____
_____

5. How has this brokenness in your relationship with God impacted other areas of your life, such as your relationships with others, your sense of purpose, or your overall well-being?

_____
_____
_____

6. Are there any specific beliefs or teachings about God that you find particularly challenging or contradictory in light of your trauma? Explain.

_____
_____
_____

7. Have you taken any steps towards healing and reconciliation in your relationship with God? If yes, describe what you have done or

are currently doing. If no, what barriers or challenges have prevented you from seeking healing in this area?

_____
_____
_____

8. What support or resources do you need to help you navigate and heal from the brokenness in your relationship with God? Consider seeking guidance from religious leaders, therapists, support groups, or other sources.

Support or resources needed:

_____
_____
_____

9. Write a prayer or a personal statement expressing your current thoughts, feelings, and desires regarding your relationship with God in light of your brokenness.

_____
_____
_____

Remember that healing is a process, and it may take time to rebuild and strengthen your relationship with God. Be patient and compassionate with yourself as you navigate through this journey. Seek support from trusted individuals or communities who can provide guidance and understanding along the way.

Effects on Self and Others:

Traumatic experiences also affect one's perception of self and relationships with others. The rupture caused by trauma can lead to a distorted self-image, feelings of worthlessness, and a diminished sense of identity. Survivors of trauma may struggle with guilt, shame, and a sense of being irreparably damaged. Furthermore, trauma often hinders the capacity to form healthy and trusting relationships, as individuals may struggle to regain a sense of safety and vulnerability in their interactions with others.

The Path to Healing and Restoration:

While trauma inflicts deep emotional wounds, theological perspectives offer hope for healing and restoration. Many religious traditions emphasize the presence of a compassionate and healing God who walks alongside those who suffer. Through spiritual practices, individuals can find solace, strength, and resilience in their faith communities. The redemptive power of religious narratives and rituals can assist in making meaning out of suffering, fostering a sense of hope, and rebuilding shattered trust.

Conclusion:

In the depths of darkness, where shadows reside,
A fracture emerges, a wound deep inside.
Trauma, the tormentor, with its ruthless might,
Shatters our world, leaving scars in its blight.

Through theological eyes, we seek to find,
The meaning behind the anguish, the reason entwined.
A rupture, a brokenness that tears us apart,
A discordant symphony within the human heart.

God, once so near, now feels distant and far,
As trauma's clutches leave us wounded, with scars.
We question the purpose, the presence of grace,
In this broken world, in this desolate space.

Safety shattered, trust turned to dust,
Existential questions, in our minds they thrust.
Who am I now, in the face of this pain?
Can I ever be whole, can I mend and regain?

But within the realms of theological thought,
A glimmer of hope, a solace is sought.
For faith can be an anchor, a steadfast guide,
Leading us through the tempest, to the other side.

In the arms of the divine, we find refuge and peace,
A balm for our wounds, a soothing release.
Strength emerges, resilient and strong,
As we journey through the darkness, singing a hopeful song.

Connections rebuild, relationships restore,
As we learn to trust again, to love even more.
Community, a salve, a balm for the soul,
Together we heal, together we're made whole.

And in this restoration, a purpose unfolds,
A sacred calling, a story yet untold.
For from the ashes of trauma, we rise anew,
With hearts that are mended, with spirits made true.

So let us embrace the journey, with faith as our guide,
Knowing that within us, resilience resides.
Trauma may wound us, but it does not define,
The strength that emerges, the light that will shine.

For through the lens of theology's grace,
We reclaim our lives, we find our rightful place.
Healing and wholeness, our ultimate goal,
As we navigate the trauma and reclaim our soul.

In the cosmic battle between humanity and trauma, the serpentine nature of trauma has sought to distort and corrupt humanity's perception of itself, God, and others. This ongoing struggle has perpetuated a cycle of suffering and disconnection.

However, amid the chaos, there are those who emerge as brave hearts, willing to confront the shadows and challenge the false performances and fleeting identities that trauma imposes. These individuals rise from the depths of their true selves, shedding the masks of pretense and embracing their authentic essence.

The journey of these brave hearts is one of self-discovery and healing. They recognize that trauma has woven a web of illusions, distorting their perception and causing them to lose touch with their inherent worth and connection to the divine. Through courage and resilience, they embark on a path of reclaiming their true identity and reestablishing their relationship with God and others.

The battle against trauma is not an easy one. It requires a deep introspection and a willingness to confront the pain and wounds that trauma has inflicted. Yet, in this struggle, the brave hearts find strength in vulnerability, compassion, and the power of community. They recognize that healing is not a solitary endeavor but a collective journey, where individuals support and uplift one another.

As the brave hearts reclaim their authentic selves, they become beacons of hope and transformation for others. Their stories of resilience inspire and empower those who have also been affected by trauma, offering a glimpse of what is possible beyond the confines of pain and suffering.

In the end, the battle between humanity and trauma is not about eradicating all suffering or completely escaping its clutches. It is about reclaiming one's power and agency in the face of adversity, and forging a path toward healing and wholeness. Through the courage of the brave hearts, humanity finds the strength to confront trauma, transcend its grip, and rediscover the profound beauty and resilience that lies within.

3 HIDDEN IN PLAIN SIGHT

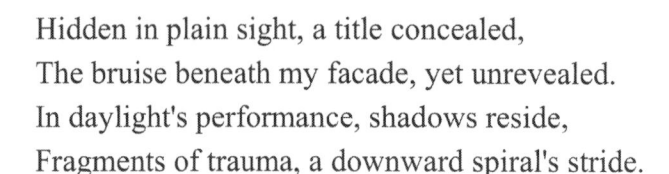

Hidden in plain sight, a title concealed,
The bruise beneath my facade, yet unrevealed.
In daylight's performance, shadows reside,
Fragments of trauma, a downward spiral's stride.

Unaddressed pain from battles fought before,
Attempts to break free, lost in abyss's lore.
The real me, restrained by time's cruel hand,
Hemorrhaging innocence, a bleeding strand.

Manifesting in all I do and say,
Invisible to all, a forest in dismay.
Can I see myself, amidst the charade,
Covering childhood horrors, emotional dress-up played.

Like a beacon of light, I yearn to be seen,
Hidden in plain sight, where my essence convenes.

Kevin Graham

Trauma can indeed be hidden in plain sight due to various factors, and the lack of action taken to address it can be attributed to several reasons. Here are some key points to consider:

If we consider the concept of invisibility metaphorically, in terms of feeling unseen, unheard, or unnoticed, there can be various causes from childhood that might contribute to such feelings. It's important to note I can provide some general information about potential causes and ways to address them. However, it's always recommended to seek the guidance of a qualified therapist or counselor for a proper assessment and personalized advice.

Causes:

1. Neglect or emotional unavailability: Growing up in an environment where emotional needs were not met or where caregivers were unavailable or neglectful can lead to feelings of invisibility. Lack of attention, validation, or responsiveness can make a child feel ignored or unseen.
2. Childhood trauma: Experiencing traumatic events during childhood, such as physical, emotional, or sexual abuse, can have long-lasting effects on one's sense of self-worth and visibility. Traumatic experiences can make individuals withdraw and feel invisible as a way to protect themselves.
3. Bullying or social exclusion: Being consistently bullied, teased, or excluded by peers during childhood can make a person feel invisible and unworthy of attention or recognition. This can impact their self-esteem and social interactions later in life.

Symptoms:

Symptoms of feeling invisible may manifest differently in individuals, but some common indicators might include:

1. Low self-esteem and self-worth.
2. Difficulty asserting oneself or setting boundaries.
3. Feelings of isolation, loneliness, or detachment.
4. Avoidance of social situations or a tendency to blend into the background.
5. Overcompensating behaviors, such as excessive people-pleasing or seeking validation from others.
6. Difficulty expressing emotions or needs.
7. Self-imposed isolation or withdrawal from relationships.

Remedies:

Addressing feelings of invisibility often requires self-reflection, self-care, and, in many cases, professional support. Here are some potential remedies:

1. Therapy: Consider seeking therapy or counseling to explore and process childhood experiences, trauma, and negative beliefs about oneself. A therapist can provide guidance, support, and tools to develop a healthier self-perception and improve relationships.
2. Self-care and self-compassion: Engage in activities that promote self-care and self-compassion, such as practicing mindfulness, journaling, engaging in hobbies, or seeking out supportive relationships. Treat yourself with kindness and compassion.
3. Assertiveness training: Develop assertiveness skills to express your needs, set boundaries, and communicate effectively. This can help you feel more visible and respected in your interactions with others.
4. Support networks: Surround yourself with supportive and empathetic individuals who validate your experiences and make you feel seen and heard.
5. Self-exploration: Reflect on your values, strengths, and interests. Engage in activities that align with your passions and help you discover your identity and goals.
6. Positive affirmations: Practice positive self-talk and affirmations to challenge negative beliefs and replace them with empowering thoughts.

Remember, everyone's experiences are unique, and the healing process takes time. It's essential to be patient with yourself and seek professional help when needed.

1. Masking and coping mechanisms: Individuals who have experienced trauma often develop coping mechanisms to help them function and survive. These coping mechanisms can include suppressing emotions, putting on a brave face, or adopting behaviors that hide their pain. This can make it challenging for others to recognize the presence of trauma.

Worksheet: Coping Skills and Strategies

Name: _____

Date: _____

Instructions: In the space provided below, list different types of coping skills and strategies that can be helpful for individuals who have experienced trauma. Provide a brief explanation or description of each coping skill.

Coping Skill 1: Deep Breathing

Explanation: Deep breathing is a relaxation technique that involves taking slow, deep breaths to help calm the mind and body. It can be useful in reducing anxiety, stress, and promoting a sense of relaxation.

Coping Skill 2: Journaling

Explanation: Journaling is the practice of writing down thoughts, feelings, and experiences in a private journal. It can provide an outlet for self-expression, help process emotions, and gain insights into one's thoughts and behaviors.

Coping Skill 3: Mindfulness Meditation

Explanation: Mindfulness meditation involves focusing attention on the present moment without judgment. It can help individuals become more aware of their thoughts and emotions, reduce stress, and enhance overall well-being.

Coping Skill 4: Physical Exercise

Explanation: Engaging in regular physical exercise, such as walking, jogging, or yoga, can help reduce stress, improve mood, and increase the release of endorphins, which are natural mood enhancers.

Coping Skill 5: Seeking Social Support

Explanation: Seeking support from trusted friends, family members, or support groups can provide comfort, validation, and a sense of belonging. It can be helpful in processing emotions and finding encouragement during challenging times.

Coping Skill 6: Engaging in Creative Activities

Explanation: Participating in creative activities, such as painting, writing, or playing a musical instrument, can serve as a form of self-expression and help individuals channel their emotions in a positive and productive way.

Coping Skill 7: Setting Boundaries

Explanation: Setting boundaries involves establishing limits and communicating them to others. It allows individuals to protect their emotional well-being and prioritize self-care by saying "no" to situations or people that may trigger or overwhelm them.

Coping Skill 8: Practicing Relaxation Techniques

Explanation: Relaxation techniques, such as progressive muscle relaxation or guided imagery, can help individuals relax their muscles and calm their minds. These techniques promote a sense of peace and reduce anxiety.

Coping Skill 9: Engaging in Hobbies or Interests

Explanation: Pursuing hobbies or interests that bring joy and fulfillment can serve as a distraction from distressing thoughts and emotions. It can provide a sense of purpose and help individuals experience moments of pleasure and satisfaction.

Coping Skill 10: Seeking Professional Help

Explanation: Sometimes, professional help may be necessary to cope with trauma. Seeking therapy or counseling can provide a safe space to explore emotions, develop coping strategies, and receive guidance from a trained professional.

Remember, coping skills and strategies may vary for each individual. It's important to find what works best for you and adapt them to your specific needs and preferences.

2. Stigma and shame: Society still carries a significant amount of stigma and shame surrounding mental health and trauma. This stigma can prevent individuals from openly discussing their experiences and seeking help. They may fear judgment, rejection, or being labeled as weak. As a result, trauma remains hidden, and people may avoid taking action due to the fear of being stigmatized.

Title: Overcoming Stigma and Shame: Promoting Mental Health Awareness

Instructions:

1. Read the provided information about stigma and shame related to mental health and trauma.
2. Answer the following questions based on your understanding and personal experiences.
3. Reflect on the strategies and suggestions provided to overcome stigma and shame.
4. Feel free to add any additional thoughts or ideas.

Stigma and Shame: Society still carries a significant amount of stigma and shame surrounding mental health and trauma. This stigma can prevent individuals from openly discussing their experiences and seeking help. They may fear judgment, rejection, or being labeled as weak.

Definition:

1. Stigma: Stigma refers to the negative beliefs, attitudes, and stereotypes surrounding a particular trait or condition. In the context of mental health and trauma, stigma often leads to discrimination, isolation, and marginalization.
2. Shame: Shame is a deep sense of embarrassment, guilt, or humiliation that individuals may feel about their mental health conditions or traumatic experiences. It can stem from internalized societal judgments and expectations.

Questions:

1. Have you ever witnessed or experienced stigma or shame related to mental health or trauma?
2. How do you think stigma and shame impact individuals' willingness to seek help?
3. What are some common misconceptions about mental health and trauma that contribute to stigma?

Overcoming Stigma and Shame:

1. Education and Awareness:

- Promote accurate information about mental health and trauma to dispel myths and misconceptions.
- Share personal stories and experiences to humanize the issue and reduce stigma.
- Encourage open discussions about mental health in schools, workplaces, and communities.

2. Language and Communication:

- Use inclusive and non-judgmental language when discussing mental health and trauma.
- Avoid derogatory terms or labels that perpetuate stigma.
- Encourage empathetic and compassionate conversations to create a safe space for disclosure.

3. Support Networks:

- Foster supportive environments where individuals can share their experiences without fear of judgment.
- Build and participate in support groups, both online and offline, that provide a sense of belonging and understanding.
- Encourage family and friends to educate themselves about mental health and offer unconditional support.

4. Media Representation:

- Advocate for accurate and sensitive portrayals of mental health and trauma in media.
- Challenge and address stigmatizing representations when encountered.
- Support media campaigns that promote mental health awareness and reduce stigma.

5. Self-Care and Self-Acceptance:

- Encourage individuals to prioritize their mental well-being and practice self-care strategies.
- Promote self-acceptance and self-compassion, helping individuals understand that their experiences do not define their worth.
- Normalize seeking professional help and therapy as an essential part of overall wellness.

Additional Thoughts:

Feel free to share any personal strategies or experiences you have found helpful in overcoming stigma and shame. Remember, breaking the silence and challenging stigma is a collective effort that benefits everyone.

Note: This worksheet is designed to encourage reflection and understanding of stigma and shame surrounding mental health and trauma. It is important to seek professional help or consult mental health experts

3. Lack of awareness and understanding: Many people lack a comprehensive understanding of trauma and its impacts. Trauma can manifest in various ways, including emotional, psychological, and physical symptoms. Without proper knowledge, it can be difficult to recognize signs of trauma in others or even in oneself. This lack of awareness contributes to the inaction and ignorance surrounding trauma.
4. Normalization of traumatic experiences: In certain environments or communities, traumatic experiences may be considered normal or even expected. This normalization can make it challenging to identify trauma since everyone around is experiencing similar hardships. Moreover, it can perpetuate a cycle of trauma as individuals may not realize that their experiences are abnormal or that help is available.
5. Apathy and bystander effect: Even when individuals do recognize signs of trauma, they may fail to take action due to apathy, lack of empathy, or the bystander effect. The bystander effect refers to the tendency for people to assume someone else will intervene or take action, leading to inaction by the group as a whole. This can be particularly problematic when it comes to addressing trauma, as individuals may assume that someone else will step in or that the responsibility lies elsewhere.

Addressing these issues requires a multifaceted approach:

a. Education and awareness: Promoting education and awareness about trauma and its effects can help break down stigma, increase understanding, and encourage early intervention. This includes providing resources and training to individuals, communities, and institutions.

b. Creating safe spaces: Establishing safe and supportive environments where individuals feel comfortable discussing their experiences can encourage disclosure and help remove the shame associated with trauma. This can be done through support groups, counseling services, and community initiatives.

c. Empathy and active engagement: Encouraging empathy and active engagement is crucial. Individuals need to be willing to listen, understand, and support those who have experienced trauma. This involves fostering a culture of compassion and providing avenues for people to access appropriate care and support.

d. Policy changes: Advocacy for policy changes at the societal level can help improve the response to trauma. This can involve pushing for improved mental health services, trauma-informed care, and legal protections for survivors.

By addressing these factors and taking proactive steps, it is possible to create a more supportive and understanding society that recognizes and responds to trauma effectively.

4 EMOTIONAL IRRIGATION
(WOUND CLEANSING)

Healing and restoration are possible, even for a wounded heart.

Once upon a time, there was a heart that had endured the brutalities of the war of life. It was battered and broken, scarred by the traumatic events it had witnessed. Unbeknownst to the heart, these experiences had left a blood clot of unforgiveness that prevented it from giving and receiving love. The heart was paralyzed by shame and regret, unable to fully embrace the beauty of love and connection.

As time went on, the heart found itself in the critical care unit of life. Abandoned, isolated, and consumed by fear, it resisted the care it so desperately needed. The heart believed that protecting itself was the only way to survive, unaware of the damaging consequences of shutting down.

However, the critical care unit understood the heart's plight. With compassion and determination, they refused to give up on the wounded heart. They hooked the heart up to an IV, allowing the fluid of love to flow through its veins once again. The team collaborated tirelessly, working together to irrigate the dirt, blood, and debris that had accumulated within the heart over time.

Day by day, the heart started to respond to the care it was given. The IV drip of love gradually thawed the clot of unforgiveness, restoring the heart's ability to forgive and be forgiven. The team worked diligently to cleanse the heart, removing the layers of shame and regret that had encased it.

As the heart collapsed under the weight of its own self-protection, it finally surrendered to the healing process. The critical care unit continued their efforts, never wavering in their commitment to bring the heart back to life.

Slowly but surely, the heart began to feel the warmth of love once again. It started to beat with renewed strength and purpose. The heart discovered that it was capable of giving and receiving love, despite the scars it bore from the war of life.

In the end, the heart learned a valuable lesson: that healing and restoration are possible, even for the most wounded souls. It discovered that love has the power to penetrate even the deepest wounds and breathe life back into a broken heart.

And so, the heart emerged from its critical care experience with a newfound appreciation for the preciousness of love. It vowed to cherish and nurture the love it had been given, and to share that love with others who were still on their own healing journey.

The moral of this story is that no matter how wounded we may be, there is always hope for healing. With the right care, support, and a willingness to let go of the burdens that weigh us down, our hearts can find their way back to love and joy.

In medical terms, irrigation refers to the process of cleaning a wound or body cavity using a stream of fluid. The purpose of irrigation is to remove debris, foreign objects, and bacteria from the wound to promote healing and prevent infection.

When paralleled with washing emotional wounds, irrigating can be seen as a metaphorical process of addressing the source of emotional wounds and cleansing them to facilitate emotional healing and growth. It involves acknowledging and understanding the emotional pain, addressing the underlying causes, and taking proactive steps to promote emotional well-being.

Emotional irrigation, also known as emotional healing, is a process that involves recognizing, acknowledging, and releasing emotional pain in an environment of self-acceptance. It is a vital aspect of personal growth and well-being, as it allows individuals to address and resolve unresolved emotional issues. By embracing emotional irrigation, individuals can experience a range of positive effects that contribute to their overall mental, emotional, and even physical health.

One of the primary reasons for embracing emotional irrigation is the need to address and heal emotional wounds. Throughout our lives, we go through various experiences that can leave a lasting impact on our emotions. These experiences may include traumatic events, losses, disappointments, or even ongoing negative patterns of thinking and behavior. If left unaddressed, these emotional wounds can fester and manifest in different ways, such as anxiety, depression, relationship difficulties, or even physical ailments.

Emotional irrigation provides a safe and supportive environment for individuals to explore and process their emotional pain. It involves identifying and acknowledging these wounds, understanding their underlying causes, and gradually releasing the associated pain. This process allows individuals to gain a deeper understanding of themselves, their emotions, and their patterns of behavior. By facing and releasing emotional pain, individuals can free themselves from the burdens of the past, leading to a sense of relief, liberation, and personal growth.

Moreover, embracing emotional irrigation fosters self-acceptance. Often, individuals carry emotional pain due to a lack of self-compassion or a sense of unworthiness. Through the process of emotional healing, individuals learn to accept themselves fully, including their emotions and vulnerabilities. They develop a compassionate and non-judgmental attitude towards themselves, allowing for greater self-love and acceptance. This self-acceptance forms the foundation for building healthier relationships, setting boundaries, and making empowered choices.

Another positive effect of emotional irrigation is the restoration of emotional balance. Unresolved emotional pain can disrupt our emotional equilibrium, causing us to feel stuck, overwhelmed, or disconnected. By engaging in the process of emotional healing, individuals can restore balance to their emotional landscape. They learn to regulate their emotions more effectively, resulting in increased emotional resilience and stability. This, in turn, enhances their ability to navigate life's challenges with greater ease and adaptability.

Furthermore, emotional irrigation can lead to improved relationships. When individuals carry unresolved emotional pain, it can impact their interactions with others. Unaddressed emotions may trigger reactive behaviors, create misunderstandings, or hinder the development of deep and meaningful connections. By embracing emotional healing, individuals can gain clarity about their emotional triggers, learn healthier ways of expressing their needs and emotions, and cultivate empathy and understanding towards others. This process can foster healthier, more authentic, and fulfilling relationships.

Emotional irrigation also has positive effects on physical health. Numerous studies have shown that emotional well-being is closely linked to physical health. Unresolved emotional pain can contribute to chronic stress, which has adverse effects on the body, such as weakened immune function, cardiovascular problems, and increased susceptibility to illness. By engaging in emotional healing, individuals can reduce stress levels, improve their overall well-being, and potentially enhance their physical health.

In conclusion, embracing emotional irrigation is essential for personal growth, well-being, and overall health. By acknowledging, addressing, and releasing emotional pain in an environment of self-acceptance, individuals can experience a range of positive effects. These include healing emotional wounds, fostering self-acceptance, restoring emotional balance, improving relationships, and even enhancing physical

Title: Emotional Irrigation Worksheet
Instructions:

This interactive therapeutic worksheet is designed to guide you through the process of emotional irrigation. By addressing and cleansing emotional wounds, you can promote healing, growth, and emotional well-being. Take your time to reflect on each question and provide honest and thoughtful responses. Remember, it's okay to seek professional help or support if needed.

Part 1: Understanding Emotional Pain

1. Describe the emotional pain you are currently experiencing.
2. What are the specific triggers or situations that exacerbate this pain?
3. How long have you been carrying this emotional pain? Is it a recent occurrence or something that has persisted over time?

Part 2: Identifying Underlying Causes

4. Reflect on the possible underlying causes of your emotional pain. This could include past experiences, relationships, unresolved conflicts, or self-perception. Write down any potential factors contributing to your emotional wounds.
5. Are there any patterns or recurring themes in your life that might be connected to your emotional pain? Consider your thoughts, behaviors, and relationships.
6. How do you think these underlying causes have influenced your emotional well-being and overall quality of life?

Part 3: Addressing and Cleansing Emotional Wounds

7. Visualize your emotional wounds as if they were physical wounds. What do they look like? How deep are they? How have they affected you?
8. Imagine a stream of cleansing and healing fluid flowing over your emotional wounds. What does this fluid represent to you? Describe its qualities and effects.
9. What steps can you take to address and cleanse your emotional wounds? Consider actions such as therapy, self-reflection, forgiveness, setting boundaries, or seeking support from loved ones.
10. Are there any specific strategies or techniques that have helped you in the past when dealing with emotional pain? If so, describe them and consider implementing them again.

Part 4: Promoting Emotional Well-being

11. How can you actively promote emotional well-being in your life? Think about self-care practices, healthy coping mechanisms, and nurturing relationships.
12. Write down three positive affirmations or statements that you can repeat to yourself during challenging times to promote emotional healing and growth.
13. Consider seeking professional help or support from a therapist, counselor, or support group. How might this enhance your emotional irrigation process?
14. Set realistic goals for your emotional healing journey. What steps can you take in the next week, month, and year to move towards emotional well-being?

Conclusion:

Remember, the process of emotional irrigation may take time and effort. Be patient with yourself as you work through your emotional wounds and seek the support you need along the way. Revisit this worksheet as often as necessary to continue your progress and promote lasting emotional healing and growth.

5 THE ANATOMY OF AN OVERCOME

In the depths of life's trials, an overcomer resides,
With courage as their armor, they fearlessly stride.
They possess the ingredients, a recipe so divine,
To transform setbacks into victories, a feat so fine.

They possess a vision that sees the unseen,
Through the darkest of nights, their spirit keen.
When others falter and lose their way,
The overcomer finds strength to seize the day.

In the realm of the unknown, they find their guide,
Unraveling mysteries, with knowledge as their stride.
With unwavering faith, they conquer the abyss,
Turning tragedy into triumph, a testament to their bliss.

Like alchemists, they turn water into wine,
Transforming the ordinary, as if by design.
Miracles flow through their fingertips,
As they walk on water, defying earthly scripts.

But it's not just magic that makes them strong,
Their resilience sings a resilient song.
They rise from the ashes, time and again,
With indomitable spirits, they transcend the pain.

Their strength is not measured by muscles alone,
It's the fire in their hearts, the spirit they've honed.
For an overcomer is defined by their will,
To rise above challenges, and their dreams fulfill.

So let us learn from these champions of might,
To face life's battles with fervor and light.
With setbacks as stepping stones, we shall ascend,
Embracing our inner overcomer until the end.

Kevin Graham

To draw a parallel between an overcomer and the anatomy of overcoming, we can explore the framework or ingredients that contribute to overcoming challenges or obstacles. Here are some key aspects:

10. Mindset: A resilient and determined mindset is crucial for overcoming obstacles. It involves cultivating a positive attitude, believing in one's abilities, and being open to learning and growth.

Description:

A resilient and determined mindset is a powerful tool for overcoming obstacles and achieving success. It involves several key components:

1. Positive Attitude: A positive attitude is essential in the face of challenges. It allows you to see setbacks as temporary and solvable, rather than insurmountable roadblocks. It involves reframing negative thoughts into positive ones and focusing on solutions rather than problems.
2. Belief in Abilities: Believing in your own abilities is crucial for building resilience. Recognize your strengths and talents, and have confidence in your capacity to learn and grow. Trust that you can acquire the skills and knowledge necessary to overcome any obstacle.
3. Openness to Learning and Growth: A resilient mindset embraces the idea that setbacks and failures are opportunities

for learning and growth. Instead of being discouraged by mistakes, view them as stepping stones toward improvement. Seek feedback, be receptive to new ideas, and continually strive to expand your knowledge and skills.

Reflection:

Take a moment to reflect on your current mindset and consider the following questions:

1. How would you describe your attitude when faced with challenges or setbacks?
2. Do you believe in your abilities to overcome obstacles? Why or why not?
3. Are you open to learning from failures and setbacks? How do you typically respond to them?

Write down your thoughts and observations:

1. My attitude when faced with challenges or setbacks:
2. My belief in my abilities to overcome obstacles:
3. My openness to learning from failures and setbacks:

Activity 1: Reframing Negative Thoughts

Negative thoughts and mental barriers can vary from person to person, but here is a list of some common examples:

1. Self-doubt: Feeling unsure about your abilities and questioning your worth or competence.
2. Perfectionism: Setting excessively high standards for yourself and feeling inadequate when you fall short.
3. Catastrophizing: Assuming the worst-case scenario in every situation and expecting negative outcomes.
4. Overgeneralization: Drawing broad negative conclusions based on limited experiences or single instances.

5. All-or-nothing thinking: Seeing things in black and white with no middle ground, leading to extreme judgments.
6. Negative self-talk: Engaging in self-critical or self-deprecating inner dialogue that reinforces negative beliefs.
7. Mind reading: Assuming you know what others are thinking about you, often assuming negative judgments.
8. Emotional reasoning: Believing that your emotions reflect reality, even when evidence suggests otherwise.
9. Labeling: Assigning negative labels to yourself or others based on specific actions or traits.
10. Personalization: Taking responsibility for events or situations that are beyond your control.
11. Discounting positives: Minimizing or dismissing positive experiences or achievements as insignificant.
12. Fear of failure: Feeling paralyzed or avoiding opportunities due to a fear of making mistakes or being judged.
13. Comparison: Constantly comparing yourself to others and feeling inadequate or resentful as a result.
14. Imposter syndrome: Feeling like a fraud despite evidence of your accomplishments and fearing being exposed.
15. Overthinking: Endlessly analyzing and overanalyzing situations, leading to increased stress and indecision.

It's important to note that everyone experiences negative thoughts and mental barriers from time to time, but if they are persistent, overwhelming, or interfere with your daily life, it may be helpful to seek support from a mental health professional. They can provide guidance and strategies to address and overcome these challenges.

Think about a recent challenge or setback you experienced. Write down three negative thoughts or beliefs that came to mind during that situation.

1. Negative thought or belief:
2. Negative thought or belief:
3. Negative thought or belief:

Now, for each negative thought or belief, reframe it into a positive, empowering statement. Focus on finding a solution or a way to overcome the challenge.

Certainly! Here's a list of reframe and positive statements:

1. Instead of saying "I can't do it," reframe it as "I haven't figured it out yet, but I'm working on it."
2. Instead of saying "I'm so stressed," reframe it as "I have the opportunity to challenge myself and grow."
3. Instead of saying "I'm a failure," reframe it as "I am learning from my mistakes and becoming better every day."
4. Instead of saying "I'm overwhelmed," reframe it as "I have many exciting opportunities, and I'll tackle them one step at a time."
5. Instead of saying "I'm not good enough," reframe it as "I have unique strengths, and I am constantly improving."
6. Instead of saying "I hate Mondays," reframe it as "Mondays are a fresh start to a productive week."
7. Instead of saying "I'm stuck," reframe it as "I'm facing a challenge that will help me develop new skills."
8. Instead of saying "I can't handle this," reframe it as "I am capable of finding a solution and overcoming obstacles."
9. Instead of saying "I'll never get it right," reframe it as "I am making progress, and each attempt brings me closer to success."
10. Instead of saying "I'm so unlucky," reframe it as "I appreciate the positive moments in my life and focus on creating more of them."

Remember, reframing negative thoughts into positive ones can have a significant impact on your mindset and overall well-being.

1. Reframed positive statement:
2. Reframed positive statement:
3. Reframed positive statement:

Activity 2: Recognizing Strengths and Talents

Identify three of your strengths or talents that have helped you overcome challenges in the past. These can be personal qualities, skills, or areas of expertise.

1. Strength or talent:
2. Strength or talent:
3. Strength or talent:

For each strength or talent, briefly describe how it has contributed to your resilience and determination.

1. Contribution to resilience and determination:
2. Contribution to resilience and determination:
3. Contribution to resilience and determination:

Activity 3: Learning from Setbacks

Think about a recent setback or failure you experienced. Reflect on the lessons you can learn from that experience and how it can contribute to your personal growth or development.

1. Lessons learned from the setback:
2. How this setback can contribute to my personal growth or development:

Conclusion:

Developing a resilient and determined mindset is an ongoing process. By cultivating a positive attitude, believing in your abilities, and being open to learning and growth,

2. Perseverance: Overcomers possess a strong sense of determination and persistence. They are willing to put in the effort and work through setbacks and failures without giving up.
3. Resilience: Resilience refers to the ability to bounce back from adversity. Overcomers develop resilience by building emotional strength, adapting to change, and developing effective coping mechanisms.
4. Support Network: Having a strong support network plays a significant role in overcoming challenges. Surrounding oneself with supportive family, friends, mentors, or a community can provide encouragement, guidance, and assistance during difficult times.

6 USING THE F WORD

The Profound Power of Forgiveness

In this chapter, we delve into the transformative concept of forgiveness—a word that carries immense weight, both in its simplicity and complexity. Forgiveness has the potential to heal deep wounds, mend broken relationships, and liberate the human spirit. It is a concept that demands exploration and understanding, as it holds the key to personal growth and emotional liberation. So, let us embark on a journey to define forgiveness, explore its various types, and uncover the remarkable benefits it bestows upon those who embrace it.

Defining Forgiveness:

Forgiveness is a profound act of releasing resentment, anger, or any negative emotions associated with a past transgression or hurtful event. It is a conscious decision to let go of grudges, bitterness, and the desire for revenge. Forgiveness is not about condoning or forgetting what has happened; rather, it is a choice to no longer allow those negative emotions to control one's present and future. It is a process that involves acknowledging the pain, understanding the circumstances, and choosing to embrace empathy and compassion.

Types of Forgiveness:

1. Self-Forgiveness: Often overlooked, self-forgiveness is a vital aspect of the forgiveness journey. It involves accepting one's own mistakes, shortcomings, and regrets, and offering oneself compassion and understanding. Self-forgiveness allows individuals to let go of self-blame and guilt, fostering self-growth and personal healing.

Introspective Worksheet: Self-Reflection and Self-Forgiveness

Instructions: Take some time to reflect on your thoughts, feelings, and experiences. Use this worksheet as a guide to delve into self-reflection and practice self-forgiveness. Be open and honest with yourself, and remember to offer yourself compassion and understanding throughout the process.

1. Self-Reflection:

   a. What are some mistakes or regrets that you hold onto? List them below.
   b. How have these mistakes or regrets affected your thoughts, emotions, and behaviors? Reflect on the impact they have had on your life.
   c. Are there any recurring patterns or themes in your mistakes or regrets? Consider if there are underlying causes or factors contributing to these patterns.
   d. How have you been treating yourself in relation to these mistakes or regrets? Have you been overly critical or judgmental? Reflect on your self-talk and self-perception.
   e. Are there any lessons or insights you have gained from these mistakes or regrets? Consider what you have learned about yourself and how you can apply this knowledge moving forward.

2. Self-Forgiveness:

   a. Acknowledge and accept your mistakes or regrets. Recognize that you are human and imperfect, and that making mistakes is a natural part of life.
   b. Understand the circumstances and context surrounding your actions. Consider the factors that may have influenced your choices and behaviors.

c. Recognize the emotions associated with your mistakes or regrets. Allow yourself to feel and process these emotions without judgment.
   d. Practice self-compassion. Offer yourself forgiveness, understanding, and kindness. Remember that you deserve to heal and move forward.
   e. Reflect on what you have learned from your mistakes or regrets. Consider how you can apply this newfound knowledge to grow and make positive changes in your life.
   f. Release self-blame and guilt. Let go of negative thoughts and beliefs about yourself. Allow yourself to be free from the burden of past mistakes.
   g. Commit to self-growth. Set intentions and goals for personal development. Focus on becoming the best version of yourself, knowing that growth is a lifelong journey.

3. Moving Forward:

   a. What steps can you take to practice self-forgiveness on a daily basis? Consider incorporating self-compassion practices, such as meditation or affirmations, into your routine.
   b. How can you use self-forgiveness to foster personal healing and growth? Reflect on the potential positive impact self-forgiveness can have on your well-being.
   c. Are there any relationships that may benefit from your self-forgiveness? Consider if there are individuals you need to forgive or seek forgiveness from, and how self-forgiveness can influence these relationships.
   d. How will you hold yourself accountable in the future? Reflect on strategies you can implement to prevent similar mistakes or regrets from occurring.
   e. What support systems or resources can you utilize to aid in your self-forgiveness journey? Consider seeking guidance from a therapist, counselor, or support group if needed.

Remember, self-forgiveness is a process that takes time and patience. Be gentle with yourself as you navigate this journey, and celebrate your progress along the way.

2. Interpersonal Forgiveness: This form of forgiveness occurs between individuals, whether it be between friends, family members, or even strangers. It involves recognizing the humanity in others, understanding their flaws and imperfections, and finding the strength to pardon their wrongdoings. Interpersonal forgiveness nurtures relationships, restores trust, and paves the way for reconciliation.
3. Transcendent Forgiveness: This type of forgiveness extends beyond personal interactions. It involves forgiving societal wrongs, historical injustices, or even forgiving oneself for the pain caused by external circumstances. Transcendent forgiveness requires a broader perspective, empathy for collective suffering, and a willingness to contribute to social healing and harmony.

Benefits of Forgiveness:

1. Emotional Liberation: When we choose forgiveness, we unburden ourselves from the weight of negative emotions. By releasing anger, resentment, and bitterness, we free up space for love, joy, and peace to flourish within us. Forgiveness promotes emotional well-being and allows us to move forward with renewed positivity.
2. Improved Relationships: Forgiveness has the power to mend and strengthen relationships. By letting go of grudges and resentments, we create an opportunity for healing, understanding, and rebuilding trust. It opens the door for authentic connections and fosters healthier, more fulfilling relationships.
3. Personal Growth: Forgiveness is an act of strength and courage. It enables personal growth by promoting self-reflection, empathy,

and resilience. Through forgiveness, we learn valuable lessons, gain wisdom, and become more compassionate individuals.

4. Physical Health Benefits: Research has shown a correlation between forgiveness and improved physical health. Holding onto grudges and negative emotions can contribute to stress, anxiety, and various health issues. By embracing forgiveness, we reduce the physiological and psychological toll on our bodies, leading to better overall well-being.

In conclusion, forgiveness is a profound and transformative act. It liberates us from the shackles of the past, enhances our emotional well-being, and fosters personal growth. It mends broken parts

Interactive Forgiveness Worksheet

Instructions: Take some time to reflect on a past transgression or hurtful event that you would like to work on forgiving. Use the following prompts to guide your thoughts and emotions. Write down your responses and explore your feelings openly and honestly.

1. Identify the person/event you would like to forgive:

[Write down the name of the person or describe the event briefly.]

2. Describe the emotions you have been experiencing in relation to this person/event:

[List all the negative emotions such as anger, resentment, hurt, etc. that you have been feeling.]

3. Acknowledge and validate your emotions:

[Write down a compassionate statement that acknowledges and validates your emotions. For example, "It is understandable that I feel angry and hurt because..."]

4. Reflect on the impact of holding onto these negative emotions:

[Think about how holding onto these negative emotions has affected your life, relationships, and overall well-being.]

5. Consider the potential benefits of forgiveness for yourself:

[Reflect on how letting go of these negative emotions and forgiving could positively impact your life, relationships, and emotional well-being.]

6. Reflect on the circumstances and perspective of the person who caused the hurt:

[Try to understand the reasons or circumstances that may have contributed to their actions. Consider their perspective, struggles, or limitations.]

7. Explore your capacity for empathy and compassion:

[Reflect on your own ability to empathize with others and show compassion. Consider how you can extend these qualities towards the person you want to forgive.]

8. Write a forgiveness statement:

[Compose a forgiveness statement that expresses your willingness to let go of the negative emotions and release the person from your resentment. For example, "I choose to forgive [person's name] and release the anger and hurt that I have been holding onto."]

9. Visualize the act of forgiveness:

[Close your eyes and visualize yourself letting go of the negative emotions and embracing forgiveness. Picture yourself feeling lighter, freer, and at peace.]

10. Commit to practicing forgiveness:

[Make a commitment to yourself to actively practice forgiveness. Write down specific actions or strategies you can employ to nurture forgiveness in your life.]

Remember, forgiveness is a personal journey, and it may take time. Be patient and kind to yourself as you navigate through the process.

Prayer of Release

Heavenly Father,

I come before You today with a heavy heart, burdened by the bruises within me. I confess my hurt, anger, and frustration that have consumed my thoughts and actions. I recognize that these emotions have hindered every aspect of my life, and I acknowledge that I am powerless to overcome them on my own. I humbly ask for Your help, Lord.

In this moment, I surrender every excuse and mental agreement that I have made with people, places, and things that hold me captive. I relinquish control and turn my will over to Your loving care for me. I understand that Your plans for my life are greater than anything I could ever imagine, and I choose to stop fighting against them. I surrender to Your divine purpose.

I let go of hate, rage, resentment, and the desire for revenge. I release all toxic ways that are counterproductive to my well-being. I choose forgiveness, Lord. I forgive all people or persons who have been involved in my perceived offenses. I drop the charges on all matters, situations, and life events that have hindered me mentally, spiritually, and relationally. I release the weight of these burdens into Your hands, trusting that You will bring healing and restoration.

Thank You, Lord, for the freedom that You bring. Thank You for the power of forgiveness and the peace that surpasses all understanding. I surrender my bruised heart to You, knowing that You are the ultimate healer. Help me to walk in Your grace and love, and to extend that grace and love to others.

In the mighty name of Jesus, I pray. Amen

ABOUT THE AUTHOR

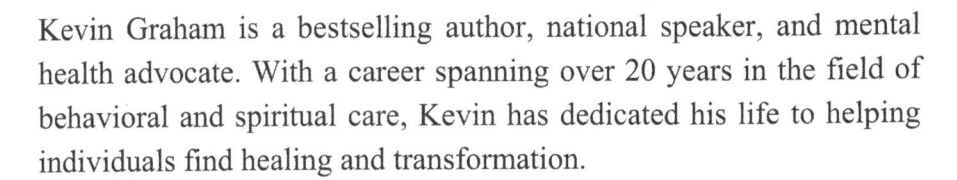

Kevin Graham is a bestselling author, national speaker, and mental health advocate. With a career spanning over 20 years in the field of behavioral and spiritual care, Kevin has dedicated his life to helping individuals find healing and transformation.

As a catalyst for change, Kevin is passionate about empowering others to overcome challenges and discover their true potential. His unique blend of personal experiences, professional expertise, and compassionate approach has made him a sought-after speaker at conferences and events nationwide.

In addition to his work as an author and speaker, Kevin is a devoted husband to his wife Monica, with whom he has shared 28 years of love and partnership. Together, they have raised three children and are proud grandparents of four.

Kevin's commitment to making a positive impact extends beyond individuals and families. He is also a dedicated reformer, working tirelessly to effect change within organizations and even on a national level. Recognizing the importance of mental health and well-being, Kevin strives to create a society that values and supports the holistic care of its members.

Through his books, lectures, and advocacy work, Kevin Graham continues to inspire and empower countless individuals, leaving a lasting legacy as a champion for transformation and a beacon of hope for those in need.

Made in the USA
Columbia, SC
02 February 2024